BEFORE YOU FLIP

How 5 investors were flipped by flipping houses and the lessons learned

---

Betty Fortune

Before You Flip
Copyright © 2020 by Betty Fortune

All rights reserved by Betty Fortune. No part of this book may be reproduced, stored in a retrieval system, or transmitted in any form or by any means, electronic, mechanical, photocopying, recording, scanning, or otherwise, except as permitted under Section 107 or 108 of the 1976 United States Copyright Act, without either the written permission from the author or publisher of this book.

Limits of Liability and Disclaimer Warranty

The author and publisher shall not be liable for misuse of this material. This book is strictly for informational and educational purposes.

Warning-Disclaimer

The purpose of this book is to educate. The author and/or publisher do not guarantee that anyone following these techniques, suggestions, tips, ideas, or strategies will become successful. The author and/or publisher shall have neither liability nor responsibility to anyone with respect to any loss or damage caused, or alleged to be caused, directly or indirectly by the information contained in this book.

ISBN: 978-0-9994622-2-5

Printed in USA by Cherokee Rose Publishing

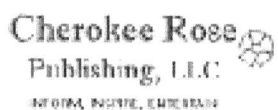

Dedication

To Hansly, my lovely husband, who has been by my side day in and day out, lifting me up and selflessly sacrificing his independent goals.

To my son, Jay, who encouraged and supported my efforts along the way.

To the memory of my father, Jean Luma, who would have been proud of this achievement.

To my wonderful brother, Kelson, who contributed to the realization of this book by sharing his experiences.

To John, my immediate younger brother, who cheered me up tirelessly throughout this process.

To the investors who agreed to share their personal stories with the world telling the good, the bad, and the ugly.

To all real estate investors and entrepreneurs across the nation. May this book serve as a compass and a prevention helping them discern a flip.

Table of Contents

Preface — 5

Introduction — 6

Chapter 1: Flip Definition — 10

Chapter 2: Unexpected Return — 14

Chapter 3: Buried Alive — 34

Chapter 4: Shoot Myself in the Foot — 49

Chapter 5: Third Degree Burn — 58

Chapter 6: Murderous Deal — 67

Summary — 78

Resources — 89

About the Author — 94

Preface

The stories recorded in this book are real-life experiences that occurred to real people. My goal in writing *Before You Flip* is to open your eyes and mind on what is happening to many investors in the real estate industry. Investors past, present, and future–my desire is for you dear reader, to not have to experience the deception, disappointment, and nightmare of living your dream of becoming an entrepreneur. Too many young entrepreneurs are being robbed, betrayed, and not compensated in recognition of their loss, suffering, or financial injuries. Although the stories here are all related to real estate, the lessons are valid for all entrepreneurs regardless of their industry.

Introduction

The day I thought I lost it all was the day I thought was my last. My hopes and dreams were crushed! The bright future I saw on the horizon faded away. My laughter quickly changed into mourning. The pain I felt was ingrained in my bones. My heart was tearing, and my soul was depressed. Like the old saying goes, robbing Peter to pay Paul…. what was I going to do?

I know real estate is a dynamic and appealing industry. Totaling up to a multi-trillion-dollar business today, real estate keeps on developing and is growing to be a fundamental piece of life. You can read about the success stories, look at advertisements, view social media, and even watch TV shows telling how individuals are creating wealth by investing in real estate. You see it constantly throughout the day, the success stories of regular hardworking people like you and me becoming millionaires through the avenue of being a real estate investor.

In fact, real estate is among the four primary wealth generators according to *Forbes* magazine. I know that this magazine is a trusted source and I do see people making it happen. Why not me? A lot of millionaires built their capital in real estate and now it was time to make mine. I was on a mission to change my financial legacy, create a steady cash flow, give back to the community, help my extended family, and be a resource to others. I knew real estate would be the key that unlocked my financial future.

We have seen the real estate market go up and down in value. However, in the past six years, the real estate market has been really heating up. It is hot and booming. More and more people have decided to invest in real estate, especially by flipping houses. I believe this has gained popularity because media outlets including TV shows, social media channels, and street signs paint the picture of a perfect real estate garden full of roses. They portray flipping houses as if it is as simple as 1, 2, 3; a way to make a quick fortune without doing much work. Many people have been fooled by offers of unrealistically high returns on their investments. Consequently, they bankrupted themselves jumping into house flipping with their eyes closed because of the glamour associated with it. That's when they are awakened by obstacles that were never mentioned or disclosed by the same media outlets claiming how simple real estate investing would be.

The purpose of writing this book is to present a balanced view of real estate investing and share with you the realities of the industry for many who at first thought this venture would change their lives. I want to address the misconceptions about house flipping as well as some common mistakes to avoid. Believing that being an investor would give them the financial resources to do so much more in their lives, people jump in headfirst not knowing how to swim the current ahead of them. You will see the reality of some everyday people with big dreams of making millions by investing in real estate.

I am sharing with you real life stories that will reveal real estate investment challenges and teach you lessons learned by people who have been through the pitfalls. You will not only learn about the obstacles, but also the lessons learned by people who faced these obstacles and failed.

To repeat Ken Schramm, "A smart person learns from his mistakes, but a truly wise person learns from the mistakes of others." Allow these stories to save you from the heartache and challenges you may face in this industry. It is important for you to be aware of and overcome these challenges. Feelings of failure or betrayal echo those of thousands of entrepreneurs and investors who continue to believe that real estate investing is a prime factor for building wealth. Like in every other industry, the general concept in today's business world "Dog eat dog" has become commonplace.

Chapter 1

Definition of Flip

According to the dictionary, *flip* is a verb that means "turn over" or "cause to turn over with a sudden sharp movement." The word *flip* originates from the 16th century. The online etymology dictionary explains how *fillip* which meant "toss with a thumb" in the 1590s eventually evolved in the 1950s to *flip* which means "go wild." In the 1690s *flip* was used to refer to "an overturning of the body or somersault."

Flip also became a word in British slang and continues to evolve. Over time, it has been used in various senses and context. For example, there are flip books, flip charts, flip coins, flip phone, etc. In the fast food industry, they flip burgers. If you pay attention to TV commercials, signs in the street, or social media posts, you may have heard about house flipping.

Flipping has become a technique used to make money. People flip furniture, collectibles, appliances, cars, or any other materials that can be bought and sold. There was even a story of a young man flipping Popeye's® sandwiches that went viral on social media. Something as simple as buying chicken sandwiches and reselling them for the double price to the customers waiting in drive thru line is a very effective way to make money while using flipping techniques. Flipping has been somewhat generalized. In today's age, people will flip anything and everything. This book focuses on "Flipology," the real estate side of flipping.

The word *Flipology* is derived from the English word *flip* and the Greek word *logos* meaning "study." Therefore, Flipology is "the science of flipping houses." This process may have several moving parts such as wholesalers, realtors, lenders, and contractors. Although they are separate entities, they interact with each other and work towards a common goal. In real estate, house flipping is when investors buy houses to sell them for a financial gain. Usually, the goal is to buy low and sell high which is the core principle of any business transaction. Some investors buy directly from the sellers, while others buy from wholesalers or the bank. To maximize their profits, investors spend money renovating most of these houses. That's when a rehab budget and a lender come into play. This budget will have a list of repairs that need to be done and the cost associated with them. The lender's job is to fund the deal.

To make money, most real estate investors follow the 70% rule in house flipping which suggests that investors pay 70 percent of the "After Repair Value" (ARV) of a property minus the cost of repairs needed. When investors buy a house, it is in its raw condition; this is the ugly side of the process. During this phase the house appears to be broken, rotten, or damaged. The goal is to flip this side and the look of the property to become so beautiful that it's irresistible to buyers. At this stage of the process, a realtor will list the fully renovated property on the market. When a qualified buyer submits an offer to purchase and successfully close the deal, the investor receives his return on investment. This business can be lucrative when you play by the rules.

A real estate investor may be an individual, a business, or other substance investing in the real estate showcase by buying, renting or in any case obtaining rights to a bit of real estate. There are a significant number of sorts of real estate investing. But house flipping is one of the most basic form of investment allowing new investors to raise capital. Remember that "basic" doesn't signify "simple." If you commit an error, the outcomes can run from minor inconveniences to severe disasters.

Chapter 2

Unexpected Return

Marie is a wife, mother of three, and a young professional in the financial industry. She is always looking for side hustles to improve her family's financial situation. She did not want to rely only on her 9-to-5 because she knew a job may pay the bills but being an entrepreneur will build wealth. The goal was to generate enough income to pay her son's college tuition, transform her life, take a hold of her finances, and ultimately create a true legacy for her family. She witnessed the real estate market crash in 2008.

On one side, many homeowners watched their home value drop to the point their loans became upside down meaning they owed more than the house was worth. They could no longer afford to pay the mortgage and their homes were foreclosed. Foreclosures and short sales were the two most popular real estate deals you could find. On the flip side, real estate investors were ready to take advantage of this market fall. They were buying inventory at a low cost and ended up making huge profits. It was a great pay period for real estate investors. The downturn was the perfect time to buy and increase assets.

Observant and aggressive, Marie's been watching the real estate market trying to understand its fluctuation for individual investors and finding a way to get involved. She was highly interested in the real estate world. She took her first step when she decided to obtain her real estate license to learn the basic principles, laws, and procedures of the industry. After obtaining her license, she worked with several real estate investors helping them secure good deals. She helped them write attractive offers to potential sellers and list these investment properties after their complete rehabs. Seeing these investors' profits increased her desire to start investing in real estate. She approached many people, seeking a mentor in order to learn the business.

In the middle of summer 2017, Marie met a guy who had been coming into her office. He was short, heavy set, and had been visiting her office for weeks negotiating checks for real estate projects. This was her opportunity; a chance to get more informed about the house flipping world. She approached him and asked about his job. She found out that he was a general contractor who had been in business for thirty years; he also mentored and coached several new investors. Marie was impressed to the point that she wanted to start working with him. It was the perfect opportunity for Marie to be coached on the investment side of the real estate business.

When Marie expressed her interest to start a mentorship with the investor, he informed her about his prices. The lowest package was $3,500. Marie was not ready to pay that price. She talked to him about her financial restrictions and he accepted to coach her with no upfront costs. They agreed on a percentage of the net profit from her first deal. Marie was excited like a kid in a candy shop. After all, he seemed to be legit. He was always professionally dressed and did not look like a typical contractor. Marie was immediately interested, scheduled several meetings with this investor mentor, learned the theories, and made several field visits observing and understanding the business. Marie was thrilled about her future in house flipping. She was ready to commit to whatever she had to do to make her first investment. She was ready to flip her first house. She was on a mission to find her first deal. She looked online and drove to different neighborhoods in search for an investment property.

Finally, in October 2018, Marie found an investment property that she wanted to invest in. After completing her due diligence, she decided to make an offer. Her real estate coach introduced her to a lender. She went through a difficult commercial loan process, although with a high interest rate. She was beyond excited. She was about to flip her first house. She was almost on her way to becoming a savvy real estate investor. As in most real estate investment loans for inexperienced investors, there is a 15% down payment required at closing. Marie did not have enough money saved. She had to take a distribution from her retirement to secure the down payment. In December 2018, she finally closed the deal and was proud to call herself a real estate investor. She thought that was the best Christmas present she had ever received. She signed the documents with her head and shoulders high, with a smile in her heart. "You become an investor when you buy," said her investor/mentor.

The deal was a super good deal. It was a bright buy! The purchase price and the rehab budget totaled $140k; the after repaired value (ARV) was $250k. It was a nice return on investment (ROI). A very good flip! Marie could picture her son's tuition paid in full, her credit card debt vanished, her broken car finally replaced, and her business flourishing. She could see her being able to quit her job soon. Being able to visualize the end brought her peace of mind and hope for a brighter future. She was so confident in this promising deal that she no longer felt the frustration of her financial stress. She was just waiting to harvest the fruits of her investment.

Soon after the project started, the investor/mentor who also played the role of general contractor was executing different parts of the budget which were not done properly. He struggled to get a rehab permit from the city. He had to use a friend's license. Marie started to question him. After thirty years of experience, he didn't have a license? He said, "Oh no, I have a license. Due to my relationship with the lender, I cannot be the general contractor in this deal. There will be a conflict of interest. I will use my friend's company on paper. But I will complete the work," said the mentor. Marie did not think anything of it. She believed in her mentor like kids believe in Santa Clause. In the budget, he did not have provisions for toilets, vanities, or heating ventilation and cooling (HVAC). He only added elements that were easy to collect money from such as landscaping, painting, and flooring. As a new investor, Marie did not know anything about what should go on a budget. Her gut feelings were telling her that something was not right. To make it worse, the lender approved the loan with the bogus budget.

Excuses, excuses, what is the delay? The contractor was talking about sick daughters and family emergencies. He began to introduce other lies to kill time. He had a range of excuses lined up. Every week was more interesting than the one before. He claimed having multiple projects that kept him busy. Some were more urgent than others. He also invented problems such as floor damages that had to be reconstructed and walls needing to be replaced; all to justify his request for more money.

He estimated the cost to rebuild the floor at $30k, which was not budgeted because it was unforeseen. Marie will have to pay him at closing. Marie was perplexed and worried about the mentor's intentions. As the rehab was progressing, the lender sent out inspectors to check out the work before funding the draw requests. Unfortunately, the inspectors did not do their job properly because all the work had to be redone. In addition, the electrician wired the house without connecting the wires, so he could pass the inspection and get paid. Sure enough, he came back later to steal the wires–so corrupt! Marie was so frustrated, she trusted in her mentor/general contractor to help her make money, not lose money with non-compliant work. Inspections were delayed and had to be repeated several times simply because the contractor did not hire professionals. He did not even pay all the subcontractors.

She felt horrible; her goal of making a good ROI was slimmed. Subcontractors were angry for not getting paid and some came back to maliciously break into the house. Others placed liens on the house. They wanted their money and rightfully so, if they completed the work. What was the general contractor doing with the funds? He was robbing Marie and the subcontractors. This was a mess! He told Marie, "Don't get discouraged, we are almost there. You just need to get another loan for me to complete the work.

I will have my friend call you to do the application," At this point, Marie did not trust him anymore. She did not get more loans to feed this crooked contractor. The investor/mentor blew out the seventy-thousand-dollar budget and Marie's pocket was bleeding! She maxed out all her credit cards trying to save the deal. She even borrowed money against her primary residence to turn the situation around. Marie decided to contact other contractors to see if she could save the deal.

Every contractor who came over was disappointed about the quality of the work being done. They even asked if she truly hired a contractor. It seemed like the work was done by a bunch of stumbling amateurs. Basically, Marie had to do everything over starting with the floor, painting, siding, HVAC, electrical, and plumbing work. In addition to that, she had to buy gutters, vanities, and toilets. The quotes to fix the house were between $40k and $60k which Marie did not have.

She contacted the lender about refinancing the loan in the hope to lower her monthly payments. She did the application and paid $600 for appraisal fees. She submitted all the paperwork that was requested to finalize this refinance. She impatiently waited for the verdict. Two days later, she received an email about the status of the refinance. She rushed to the end of the email, but it was the appraisal report. The value of the house was now $300k. That made Marie's heart smile again.

She continued to wait for the final decision. She called the lender and sent emails. Finally, she received a second email from the lender. She could not wait to open it. Surprisingly, her refinance request was denied because the house was not in a livable condition. The lender asked Marie to rewire the house to make sure the electricity was on and purchase vanities and kitchen appliances before they send out an inspector to confirm the house condition. Marie was disappointed. She could not believe this. She contacted several other lenders looking for a different outcome, but she received the same answers.

Marie and her family were brainstorming about how to exit the deal. Since the value was still there, they opted to tackle different parts of the project individually. They chose to hope again and decided to hire separate subcontractors to help finish the project. They hired a painter, a floor technician, a plumber, and an electrician to make it happen. The project was back to life.

When Marie contacted the city for final inspection, they told her she had to re-permit the project because twelve months had already passed. All the rough inspections had to be redone. She was devastated and plunged into despair. She thought she was trapped in a dead-end deal. She felt as if she was torn in half. After several nights of insomnia, thinking about what to do, Marie chose to go back to the lender one more time. She requested a deed in lieu of foreclosure which is a process where the homeowner voluntarily transfers the property title to the lender in exchange for a release from the mortgage loan. She wanted to get out, to cut her losses. She wanted to pull back and shut everything down. However, her family did not support this decision knowing the impact it would have on her credit score. Giving up was not an option. It was like world war three in the family; they could not agree on this.

After having calmed discussions, Marie conceded and accepted to consider other options although she did not feel there were any other options left. That's when she started to look for other investors interested in partnering with her by investing in the new repair cost and sharing the profit. That was a brilliant idea! She got excited again. She contacted three different investors who started to evaluate the project. They sent their contractors and appraisers out to look at the property. They gave Marie hope. She waited and waited. At the end, none of them moved forward with the partnership.

Marie's entire family was looking for a potential savior. In one of their brainstorming sessions, she and her family decided to sell the property as is. For the third time, she went to the lender, this time to ask about the balance owed. She was actively looking for an investor who was willing to resuscitate the project and pay the balance of the mortgage. A lot of investors' offers were significantly below the market value. They were low-ball offers.

Finally, she was able to find a reasonable investor willing to buy the property. Marie did not believe it until she was at the closing table handing the keys over. That's how Marie got out of this financial jail. She could not believe that she was finally free.

Marie's mentor contacted her when he realized the house was sold. He had the nerve to ask Marie when she was going to pay him the $30k he spent out of pocket on the floor. Marie asked him to discuss this in front of a judge. She never heard back from him.

This toxic situation had led to depression, anxiety, and other medical problems. Marie had always had perfect blood pressure. She was healthy like a horse. After going through so much, Marie's hair started to fall out, her blood pressure was higher than normal, and her weight was uncontrollable. Her emotions would rise and fall, twist and turn. Instead of flipping the house, she was flipped!

Marie went through all the trials and tribulations that came with the daily grinds of doing a house flip. One bad contractor flipped the entire situation. As time went on, she progressively lost confidence in the profitability of her investment. She had to continue to make the monthly payments until the house was transferred to another investor.

The goal was to add a new stream of income, but it ended up adding another huge expense on the family budget that ate up her entire salary which made it impossible to pay bills and face other financial obligations. She felt guilty as she questioned her decision to jump into the house flipping business. Late payments started to pile up which impacted her credit score.

Money was less flexible. She did not have any funds left after she paid for the investment home and her primary residence mortgages. All the unexpected expenses associated with the investment property were added to Marie's list. She was under water. Because she had to deal with so many financial struggles, it was difficult to have both ends meet. This situation had a direct effect on her family, especially on her husband.

Now, he had to step up to the plate and make sacrifices because of her financial shortcomings. He had to take a second job just to cover the bills. He had less time to spend with the family and was frustrated at times. He sometimes got mad when he realized they were unable to save money as usual. He often complained about not being able to please his children. All his money was going towards this dead deal. He was tired of working hard for nothing. He worked around the clock. He could never talk to his friends. Every time they called him, he told them, "I am at work, can't talk right now," but whenever they asked him to borrow $50, he never had any money. He was always working and always broke.

Marie had a self-condemning heart. She was swallowed up by guilt because she put her husband through all that turmoil. Her baby could not go to day care because she could not afford it. Her family suffered because of her decisions. Marie was mentally impacted. She took responsibility for what was happening to her family. She started to look for part-time jobs to help pay the bills.

Looking back, there were many red flags along the way that warned her that this contractor/mentor shouldn't be trusted. His priority was to fill his pocket by extorting others. He often said, "I am going to get everything out of this budget" without focusing on the quality of the work being done. It took him days to answer a simple question and he was dishonest about basic things. Again, red flags, but Marie was not listening; she was blindsided. The basic principle of flipping houses was to get in and get out quickly. We know time is of the essence in this business.

At the beginning, Marie expected a financial gain to better her family because money is very important in these days we live in. Without money one can be forced to live a different life that can eventually bring issues. At the end, she gained something much more important.

- First, she gained experience. She knows what not to do, how to spot the red flags, and the tricks of the business. Her patience was tested big time! Waiting vainly for eighteen months requires a lot of patience. The knowledge gained from this experience helped her make better decisions in her other deals.
- Second, this situation brought her family together. Her son and husband were often together brainstorming a way out or strategizing ways to cut losses. Her teenage son renounced his prom and homecoming to allow his mom to afford to pay the mortgage. He was missing out on activities and celebrations he took for granted like a birthday party. Whenever he needed something, he had to ask in advance so it could be accounted for in the budget. He learned how to prioritize and ask for what he re-

ally needed over what he wanted. The coherence and love among the family members was stronger. Although she did not gain anything financially, what she got was priceless. The profit she would have made could not buy patience, humility, passion, experience, and inspiration. It could not reinforce the bonds in her family. Marie realized the best things in life *are* free. Her happiness is not related to her financial status. She thought paying off debts or buying a new car would make her happy. But, the love, modesty, and spirit that reigns in her family makes her one million times happier. With her family support, Marie was able to cope with the worst experience she had ever had. Although she was shaken by several trials, she retained her inner peace. Here are some things to consider before you jump into a deal that can affect your well-being:

- Money is not everything; never go into a deal without a purpose. Always have a master plan and a backup plan, especially if you are new to the industry.

- Make sure you are ready financially and mentally. Plan for the unexpected. Be sure to have some cash reserve to cover at least ninety days of expenses including the monthly mortgage. Consider potential consequences on your mental health if the deal goes left.
- Never jump into a deal without a parachute. Having some savings in place or set aside for your business can protect you from similar situations that Marie had to experience.
- Always trust and verify. Remember you are putting your business name, credibility, and hard-earned dollars into this investment. You are taking full responsibility for this transaction. Make sure you can trust everybody you are working with, so everything runs smoothly.

Not only do you have to be confident that your contractors and subcontractors can perform the job, but you also should feel good about their integrity and work ethic. You want to make sure they will not backstab you by taking advantage of you and your situation. They know how to manipulate the system to benefit themselves. Be sure to partner with people who will put their best foot forward. Otherwise, you will have a snowball effect where your monthly mortgage payments will continue with no end in sight.

Chapter 3

Buried Alive

Kelly and his wife are newlyweds who share common ideas and ambitions for the future. As a young couple, they love to travel and have visited many different countries. Besides traveling, they enjoy spending time together and doing many things together. They complement each other very well. One of their main goals was to go into business as a couple. They always wanted to combine their strengths, skills, and life experiences to create a successful investment company and serve as role models for the younger generation.

For the past six years, they have been interested in different types of investments, mainly real estate. They've talked about having rental properties in addition to owning their first home to create residual income. They were excited to purchase their first residential home in 2012. They were more excited when they saw how quickly the equity in their house increased. Looking at the equity that had accumulated on the house in such a short period of time, they thought about what they could accomplish with the equity. They decided to sell their first home and expand by purchasing a bigger and nicer home. This experience was fantastic. They sold their first home to a real estate investor. They made money from the sale of their first home and were able to pay down some of their debts and finance the down payment on a second home. They were thinking, "Man, we can duplicate this process and make more money." They were determined to start a business in the real estate industry.

Looking back, they remembered the first time they were exposed to real estate investing. They heard a commercial on the radio promoting a two-day conference in Atlanta. They signed up and were in attendance. They were excited about the knowledge, the many success stories, and were inspired to continue on their journey. On the first day, they learned about starting a real estate career–the ups and downs. On the second day, they were introduced to a program that teaches people how to flip houses and gives them the tools and resources they can use to succeed. The cost of this program was between $15k and $30k. After being interviewed, because you must be "interviewed" to be selected, they were "qualified." Only a few people qualify to get into the program, according to the organizers. The organizers want to make sure they recruit the right people.

They were thinking, "Oh wow, we have to do really well since the organizers will only select a few people to get into the program. We cannot afford to be left behind; we need to start investing right away. They were selected for the program and were proud and excited. As soon as they were accepted into the program, they were expected to pay the minimum enrollment fee of $15k the same day. They thought this was ridiculous and stupid. They refused to pay that much. At this point, the lady who was signing them up made a smart comment that made them feel almost like they let their family down by not taking advantage of the program.

In Kelly's head, he was like, "I don't necessarily need your program to be successful. In addition to that, you don't know anything about me. Why would she even make a comment like that?" They quickly understood that she was just there to sell them a package.

Although they skipped this opportunity, in the back of their minds, they always thought that real estate investing was the route they wanted to take. Initially, they were thinking about starting with a small deal. They knew they had to have enough money saved up to buy an investment house. They had multiple conversations about real estate investing. They successfully performed their first flip, they thought about their first home, which they sold in 2016. Selling their first home and using the profit to pay their debts and finance the down payment on a second home was inspiring. After this transaction, they were convinced and ready to get started.

To help facilitate the transactions and maximize profit, Kelly's wife obtained her real estate license. She was now a licensed realtor and had access to different lists of investment properties. That's when their passion started. Their experience as homeowners was the main reason they decided to start flipping houses. "We thought it was a process that was relatively easy to do and make a profit," said Kelly's wife.

They knew for a fact that they wanted to have their own investment business and a part of it had to do with real estate, of course. Getting into real estate was the foundation to start building capital and some sort of revenue to expand their vision. They started an investment company and went through the process of state registration. They have had conversations with other investors to include his mom and one of his sisters. That's when his sister told him about this real estate investor who appeared to be successful; it might be a way to learn the process. Maybe he could introduce this couple to the house flipping world. Kelly decided to go meet this investor and had a long conversation about what he does. After the conversation, the guy reached out to Kelly and said, "I understand you want to get into real estate. I want to show you what I've been doing." Kelly drove to see some of his previous flipping projects. He talked about his successes and how long he had been in the business.

In addition to that, he mentioned how he used some of the profit from flipping to open a new restaurant. Kelly was thinking, "Wow, this dude truly knows what he's doing." He was impressed by what he saw. Obviously, the new restaurant was not making that much money. The owner must have some type of additional income to sustain. Kelly's assumption was based on the fact that this real estate investor was successful. Kelly saw, in this guy, who he wanted to become and thought he would be a great person to simply learn from-a great way to network and get his feet wet. He started to trust this investor and decided to jump in.

Starting out, Kelly invested in an existing project that needed some minor cosmetic work according to the investor. When Kelly went to the site, he confirmed the good condition of the house. No additions or major repairs were necessary. All the investor needed was some cash to fix the house and in three months it would be on the market and they would make some money. They discussed the numbers, and everything made sense. They decided how the profit would be divided. Kelly thought it was a smart idea and felt good about the deal.

In fact, the house was in an excellent school district, great neighborhood, and solid "comparable." The fact that the investor said he already owned the property; it should have been a win-win situation. With his experience, if he said it would take $20k to fix the property, that's it. It should have been good to go! With no second thought, the couple poured in the $20k. After the investment, things didn't go as planned in terms of timing. Timing is very important for a real estate investor because the less time you spend investing in a property, the higher your return on investment.

The couple started to see some red flags when the process took longer than expected. After two months, no progress had been made. The couple had to drive an hour and a half (one way) once a month to view the property just to realize that nothing was moving as it should after they invested their cash.

When the couple asked the investor what was going on, he acted like he was shocked to hear it. "What? The contractor has not been there this week? I'll get on him," replied the investor. Basically, it was a bunch of nonsense. Something always happened. Every other day it was something else. A tree fell, the weather was bad, etc. The couple insisted that it didn't make any sense. For someone with his experience, they thought he should already have a strong reliable team in place, based on previous projects he had done. There is no reason why a contractor does not do the work if he's getting paid. The couple decided to get the contractor's contact information to stay on him personally. To be honest, the couple was very passive with that and did not follow up with the contractor. They were relying on the investor just because he lived closer to the property. However, the investor lied throughout the whole process. He never used any of the money towards repairs.

Months went by and nothing happened. The renovation was never completed. Things didn't go as planned; however, the couple did not give up. In lieu of the pitfalls of this project, while waiting for the rehab to be finished, they decided to buy a property under their business name and try to do a house flip on their own.

This time they were paying the mortgage, dealing with the contractor, and basically had more control. They felt good about the potential profit margin and got excited again. They were sure they would be able to build credibility. This time they had the funds to do the work. They partnered with the investor, giving him a chance to redeem himself hoping he would deliver on his promises. Kelly and his wife trusted the investor, gave him a second chance, and partnered with him on the next deal. It seemed like everything was going smoothly. He spent the money allocated to the repairs and this time, there was a potential buyer who advanced some funds towards the completion of the house.

This was very promising–or so Kelly thought; a potential buyer who paid money up front to complete the house! But to no avail, the investor pocketed the money and used it between the restaurant and his personal financial obligations. Now, the buyer sued Kelly for mismanagement of funds. Kelly was in disbelief again; this investor was stealing the money again. They had given him the benefit of the doubt and entrusted him with their hard-earned money, all that they had saved to make their dream of being a successful real estate investor a reality. And that thief used the money for his own personal gain–unbelievable! They found out that the investor had been using other people's money to finance his restaurant business. Then he would use the additional income to invest in minor repairs/projects on the property; just enough to keep them interested. He was literally stuffing his pockets with their money.

Kelly and his wife suffered financial loss because they fell for this scam! This situation led to several late payments impacting their credit score. They struggled to respond to their basic financial needs. They could no longer afford to travel as they used to. They had to reduce their outings and were facing various societal stresses and strains. It was devastating.

All their life savings was invested in these properties and they were buried in a deep financial hole with an impossible amount of debt. They felt suffocated by financial woes and emotional distress. Finally, they could no longer afford the payments on those mortgages and had to face foreclosure. They soon had the worst credit history they ever had in their lifetime. Foreclosure can stay on your credit for up to seven years.

The feelings were indescribable. The financial anxiety, the pressure, and the emotional stress were a form of torture that made each passing day a trial. They could not see a way to climb out. In their financial dark hole, they were more than six feet under. They were covered with debt, bad credit, lawsuit, worries, and losses. Even now, heartache and deep emotional pain occasionally strikes. They ended up flushing over $60k down the drain. They were buried alive. They were flipped.

From all of this, it is not just about real estate. It rings true for any business partnership. Whenever you are getting involved or building any type of relationship with anybody, you should look for common characteristics and values. Looking back on this experience, Kelly feels like he failed to investigate that further. There are certain things he values as a man and a husband that the investor did not value at all whether it is from a spiritual standpoint or a man of character.

Because the couple was more focused on the big picture, which was the financial aspect of their investment, they did not pay enough attention to the little things about the investor's personality. Those things included being a person of integrity and being a natural liar and manipulator. The couple had seen some red flags along the way that they simply chose to ignore because they were focused on the aspect of trying to make more money. They were consumed by the things they thought they had to have to be happy and successful. They did not let this financial crisis put their marriage in shambles, eroding their love. They learned how to rely on each other, be creative, and use simple activities they can do together to bring joy and happiness. They also learned how to appreciate the simple and most important things in life.

From this experience, they learned how knowing your partners is a vital part of a successful business. If you're going to have any type of business relationship with anybody, it's very important to test that person's integrity and character. If there are any red flags, do not ignore them as you will never be able to ignore the negative consequences and build a long-term relationship. You are taking too much of a risk. Partner with people you can trust. Make sure you do your due diligence and check their references. Before you know if someone is the right partner, you need to know who you are first.

Self-awareness is so important in business decisions; it is crucial. Know the different facets of your personality including your strengths, weaknesses, beliefs, mannerisms, habits, interests, motivation, short comings, and emotions. When you understand yourself then you can understand your work ethic and be more productive. By becoming more self-aware and recognizing your strengths, weaknesses, and hidden biases, you can decide which partner suits your personality and business style the most. Self-awareness will support your success.

Secondly, invest in yourself more. Educate yourself, so you don't have to rely solely on somebody else to do everything for you. Learn as much as you can about the industry you are interested in. The thing about getting from step A to Z, is that sometimes we want to take a shortcut. But there is no shorter way; you must go through the process. Don't skip any phases. Otherwise, you'll pay for it towards the end. Plus, you'll have to go back and repeat every step.

Thirdly, in the process of doing deals, have contracts in place defining the scope of the work. Do not invest more than you can afford to lose. Never jump blindly! Risk management is a critical skill to develop as entrepreneurs. Going through hardships can only improve one's understanding of themselves and gain experience that no one besides life can teach you.

Chapter 4

Shoot Myself in the Foot

Born and raised in Georgia, Andrew was not a typical teenager. He grew up with an entrepreneurial mentality. Since high school, Andrew was highly interested in entrepreneurship. He enjoyed reading investment books and dreamed about becoming a successful businessman. He did a lot of research and attended several seminars attempting to learn the best ways to invest. He became more engrossed in studying a variety of offerings and market reports. He was actively looking for ways to invest.

He envisioned financial freedom at an early age; he never pictured himself making someone else's dreams come true. While his friends were preparing for college and working part time jobs, he was working on buying a Subway® franchise at only 18 years old. His mindset was focused on creating wealth through investments, especially in real estate.

At 19 years old, using his savings and money borrowed from lenders he purchased his first investment home, applied the concepts learned from books, and was able to successfully flip the property and make a small profit. It wasn't bad for a first deal. From this point, Andrew was confident about his future in the business. He was well off on the winning track. His mindset, attitude, and motivation played a critical role in his journey. He certainly had his foot in the right direction; that was a great way to get the ball rolling.

Without a doubt, his success was promising. He had already gotten a taste of success and was hungry for more. That's why he was searching for a mentor who could take his success to the next level. He took some small steps such as participating in several networking events, spreading the word through friends, and using social media. He was skeptical about choosing the right mentor.

One Saturday morning, he went to get a haircut at his favorite barbershop. That's where his barber introduced him to this wonderful contractor who was going to help him with his project. Although a contractor isn't necessarily a mentor, nonetheless he was someone who could help Andrew maximize his profit. Since this was a warm referral from a barber that he trusted, he did not question the contractor's ability or integrity. He extended the trust he had in his barber to this contractor he had just met.

Andrew purchased a beautiful home that required little to nothing to be fixed. The house was gorgeous, spacious, and well maintained. It was in a perfect location within a great school district. Andrew even had a potential buyer waiting for the minor repairs to be made. They agreed on the purchase price and it was simply a waiting game. Andrew was excited to meet this contractor and agreed to work with him. He invited the contractor to examine the project to see how much the rehab would cost. The contractor went to the house to see what needed to be done, then gave Andrew a budget and timeframe to complete the project. The numbers made sense and they signed a contract.

Andrew purchased all the materials and had them delivered on site. Three days after the start date agreed upon, to Andrew's surprise, the project hadn't commenced. In the meantime, Andrew noticed that some of the materials were missing. The contractor didn't keep his word on the timeline and was lying about small simple things. He was constantly making excuses for why the project was delayed.

One day, the contractor came to Andrew and told him, "Man, my wife loves this house. We want to rent it from you." Shocked, Andrew asked him, how he was going to afford the monthly payments. This was a big jump compared to what they were currently paying. And more to the point, Andrew already had a buyer. In the back of his mind, Andrew was worried about how the wife got involved. When did she see the house to fall in love with it? He started to question the contractor's integrity. Nevertheless, Andrew gave him the benefit of the doubt and wanted to keep the agreement they had made. The contractor begged him to agree to rent the house. He talked about how his wife would generate income from her new job. He acted in a way that made Andrew feel guilty about not helping a family in need. To make it worse, he didn't have the down payment (deposit). He proposed to fix the house as the price of his labor, using the materials that were already on-site.

Andrew felt bad for him and his family. Even though the request made no sense and was unrelated to the original contract, Andrew granted him the favor of renting the house. They had a deal. Andrew fell for the banana in the tailpipe. The contractor and his family moved into the house. The first month came, but Andrew didn't receive the rent payment. After contacting the contractor, he told Andrew he was having a hard time and financial difficulties. But he promised to do the impossible, to pay the next month and catch up. Second month came, no payment. It was another set of problems.

On top of that, the contractor was complaining about extra repairs that needed to be done. Note, these repairs were not mentioned in the original scope of work. Andrew had to come out of his pocket to pay the mortgage a second time which he wasn't prepared to do. The third month passed by, still no payment.

This time, he blocked Andrew's phone number. He was unresponsive. There was not a way of communicating with him. At this point, Andrew had to refer to the court system to evict him. This process took over 30 days. All the costs involved came out of Andrew's pocket. The contractor was finally evicted; the house left deteriorated and falling apart. The walls had plenty of holes. He didn't do any of the repairs he promised to do in exchange for his down payment. He dishonestly feigned interest in the rehab project. The materials were gone. Andrew had to use several credit cards to pay for materials and certain bills. They were maxed out. The compound interests were outrageous. Andrew had to apply for a store credit card to buy the materials again and hired someone else to do the original repairs and the damages caused by the contractor.

This young investor was facing serious financial issues due to these unexpected expenses. During that time, Andrew had to continue to make the mortgage payments to avoid losing the property. He had to get a loan to help cover these expenses. He lost his savings and his investment home. Andrew was financially drained. His cash flow diminished, his margin profit was ruined, and his dream was crushed. He was flipped!

Nevertheless, this relationship took even more of a downward turn. Since they both used the same barber, the contractor was always threatening Andrew and held him accountable for what his family was going through. Andrew became the bad guy. Things became sour. It was always a confrontation every time they both were there at the same time. One day, the contractor pulled out his gun to shoot Andrew. He had to fight for his life!

In the end, Andrew almost lost his life over a flip. He truly shot himself in the foot. Looking back, he recalled the simple lies, the stolen materials, the questionable behaviors, and the way the contractor treated the subcontractors. Andrew ignored these signs and didn't take them seriously. This flip that had so much potential turned out so very wrong. The contractor stayed in the house over four months for free, with no down payment. Andrew was flipped in this transaction. He ended up facing foreclosure and lost the property. It took him years to bounce back.

Despite this negative experience, Andrew learned the importance of doing your due diligence every time you are dealing with a contractor or business partner. Stop extending trust to complete strangers. Your trust should be earned not transferred. Perform a background check if necessary, and read their reviews. Hire the right people; those who have something to lose such as their reputation, license, etc.

Stop trying to save a few bucks by hiring Joe down the street. Never ignore the red flags. When someone shows you who they are, trust them. You will avoid being shot in the foot. In any project, skills and knowledge converge, relationships improve, as does the general mood and they will continue to enrich themselves.

Unity is strength in pursuing a common goal, a priceless added value that should not be underestimated. That's why we should work on ourselves and improve some aspects of our character to enhance productivity and create a winning team. Then, start working on self-awareness, self-knowledge as a person, knowledge of our skills, and self-view as others see us. Only after having a greater understanding of our values, but also our limits, can we meet excellent teamwork. Being empathetic is great, but not to the point of shooting yourself. An entrepreneur must be aware of, first, himself/herself and the people that he or she is working with in order to obtain maximum results.

Chapter 5

Third Degree Burn

Daniel, a middle-aged family man, is a retired Army veteran with a wife and two children. He was honorably discharged from the U.S. Army in 2016 after 25 years of service. After returning from Vietnam, he felt the need to make an impact in the community. He brought with him memorable adventures-some painful and others courageous.

The transition to civilian life was not easy. He attended different workshops designed to help his adjustment be smooth. In his desire to continue to serve, he joined the local police department to continue his mission to protect and serve. Deep inside, he was always attracted to real estate. He read a lot of books and watched many TV shows related to flipping houses. He wanted financial stability for his family.

His goal was to contribute to the wealth of his community by providing affordable housing to low income families. For him, flipping homes was not only about making money. It was mainly about helping low income families achieve the American dream without breaking the bank. Affordable housing was his priority. That was his new purpose. He wanted the underprivileged to have some level of comfort without paying a luxurious price. He was searching for a real estate coach to help him on this journey.

Somehow, he reconnected with a long-time friend who was in the army with him years ago. This friend identified himself as a real estate mentor/contractor. Daniel was beyond happy! He couldn't believe his luck of reconnecting with the right person. He thought God had answered his prayers. He was sold. He could smell the success awaiting him.

Although he hadn't seen this friend for years due to the distance between them, he remembered the 20 years of friendship and their challenges in Vietnam and Iraq. It was a great reunion. Daniel shared his dream of becoming a real estate investor. The friend promised to coach Daniel and teach him everything he needed to know about real estate investing.

Daniel was determined to jump into real estate right away. He immediately quit his job as a police officer to begin his real estate investor journey; he was that serious. He wanted the time to focus on his project with no distractions. He walked away from a full-time job that was paying the bills to walk through a door that would fulfill his dream. His wife was very optimistic and supportive; she felt Daniel's passion and dedication. She had no doubts about his plan's success. She knew her husband would continue to provide and support the family. A brighter future was on the way.

Daniel had to jump through some hoops and get past a few roadblocks before he received the approval to finance his first project. He had some credit challenges, but he did it; he was finally at the closing table. He sealed the deal and was ready to start. But what happened next shook him up.

His contractor friend was helping manage the project. The first phase (demolition) went well. Right after, Daniel didn't like the way his contractor was handling the project. His way of doing business was questionable. He had a shady character and dragged his feet to complete simple work. His reputation was tarnished. He was known for not paying his subcontractors. In fact, he hired people off the street as subcontractors. Therefore, they did a poor job. Materials were stolen on-site, the house was vandalized, and the electrical wires were stolen. The contractor blew up the entire budget without completing the job properly. A project that was supposed to be completed in 8 weeks took 12 months.

Daniel ended up firing the contractor friend, hired another contractor, and borrowed thousands of dollars to complete the project. The friendship was deteriorating. Basically, Daniel had to repeat most of the work. Every first of the month, he had to make the mortgage payment. He was relying on this quick flip to provide for his family and finance a second project, but he got burned. He was flipped.

The damages were not superficial. They will be felt forever and ultimately destroyed his dream. They had progressed to impact his household. It was deep. These are the traits of a third-degree burn. A third-degree burn may heal on its own, but the process takes a long time. This project was his only source of income. As the only breadwinner in the family, he was unable to put food on the table. His plan to provide for his wife and children was shipwrecked.

Reality started to kick in. He worked every day trying to expedite the process. He had depleted his savings to save the deal. The savings that was dedicated to his daughter's college tuition had vanished. His quality of life began to suffer. He was physically and mentally drained, incapable of facing his responsibilities as a father and a husband; it burned his soul. He was stressed out to the point that steam was coming out of his ears. This smoke became a major fire that ravaged this family financially. This burning almost prevented Daniel and his family from continuing to dream big and forced them to scale back their vision and settle with something that was not what they really wanted. He had to face his wife and explain to her how wrong he was.

She was very understanding. His wife started to think about getting a job, but she had always been a stay-at-home mom. It was difficult for her to step out. Since she didn't have any work experience, she was having a difficult time finding a job. She was turned down after countless interviews. Daniel and his wife fell victim to failure and were left with a terrible sense of unworthiness. She wanted to rip her hair out. She patiently endured all those torments and was a real support to Daniel throughout the entire time.

Daniel had to wear multiple hats and do some of the rehab job himself. He had to roll up his sleeves and use some of the construction skills he learned in the military. He was on-site seven days a week working on completing the project. In the end, they were able to sell the house, but there was no profit. He lost time and money. He was flipped.

Daniel learned a lot from this experience, such as:

- Make sure you inspect what you expect.
- Never let a contractor handle a project without supervision. At the end of the day, the contractor is working for you. A strong presence on-site is essential because it gives you more control.
- Stop the contract as soon as you see a red flag. These red flags are flammable and can be caught on fire very quickly. Don't get burned, use caution.

Everywhere in the world, red lights are associated with stop. Stop and cut your losses. Do not be these people who literally stop trying to achieve their goals because they are so afraid of failing or being perceived as a failure. Most people who are successful will probably testify to the number of times they have made an attempt at being successful in an endeavor. At least they tried and learned where they went wrong to be better prepared for the next attempt. They often feel ashamed in asking for help but that is one of the greatest gifts to have and that is to know when you may need assistance and realizing it is not a sign of weakness but actually showing strength and reasoning to seek assistance sometimes.

In addition, know where to draw the line between friendship and business. Not all friends can be business partners. By knowing the borderlines of your actions, you will be able to balance investments and relationships. Like many entrepreneurs, this project has cost him his friend.

Afterwards, people change at any time. When you go years without seeing some friends, do not assume they have the same values. You have no idea of what they've been through or their current circumstances which can alter their personality. You don't know whom they have become. Before resuming the friendship, make sure they are still the same friend you have known throughout of the years.

Finally, never give up. Although Daniel was flipped doing his first deal, he continued to build on this failure and was able to flip several houses successfully. He was able to build a great team. He's fulfilling his mission to provide affordable housing to low income families.

Chapter 6

Murderous Deal

Jamie is a very sought-after young man who is a successful realtor living in Washington, D.C. Many girls would like to marry him, but still, he has no wife, kids, or pets. He had a girl in mind at one time. The problem was not having enough money. The wedding plans had to be delayed time and time again. Therefore, he was always looking for opportunities to expand his business to other states in the south, especially Atlanta.

After getting hurt in a car accident, he received some financial compensation. He did not want to spend all the money and end up broke within a few months. Although he was undecided on how he would invest the settlement, he knew that he wanted to do something that would create passive income-enough to allow him to marry the love of his life and live comfortably. In fact, he proposed to his longtime girlfriend and planned on having a memorable wedding on the beach. At first, he thought about saving for retirement. He wanted to invest the money in a way that would guarantee an early retirement. After doing a lot of research on how to invest for retirement, he came across an article on real estate investment. The article was interesting and triggered his interest in investing in real estate.

He started to look at different markets that would have been ideal for his investment. A few cities were on the growing market list And Atlanta was at the top of the list. He was seriously thinking about flipping a house in Atlanta. However, he did not know much about Atlanta and he was afraid to fail. Taking that step was very difficult for him because of the embarrassment of failure. He was not sure if it was the best course of action to take. He was afraid to act. He was up and down like a roller coaster ride until he could figure out which route to take.

He decided to visit Atlanta a few times just to meet the right people and to see if there were opportunities for real estate investment. His mind was blown away by the activities, transaction volume, and number of deals. The real estate market was hot. Everybody was moving to Atlanta. The cost of living was reasonable, and the opportunities were unlimited. He automatically understood why Atlanta was known as "Hotlanta." He was convinced about investing in Atlanta.

Jamie did not have prior knowledge or experience in the flipping industry. Therefore, he was looking for strong partners who could help him get in and out quickly. His goal had two parts which included finding an investment property and hiring a contractor. He started to work on the first part of his goal. He was online looking for great listings and drove to different streets in the city of Atlanta looking for potential deals.

That's when a nice duplex sitting on the curve of this historic neighborhood caught his eyes. It was a raw diamond in the heart of Atlanta. He could imagine how he was going to transform this duplex into a masterpiece. He envisioned the architecture, color, and design. He was able to locate the seller and paid $60k cash for the property. He jumped on it and closed the deal. He and his fiancée were so excited. They knew this deal was the beginning of the future they wanted for their family. They dreamed about the potential return on this investment. They were off to a great start. Now, he was ready to move to the second part of his goal which was to find the right contractor. He met with several contractors, but he did not know who to trust. He wanted the best for this project, and he was looking for someone who could bring his vision to life. He was ready to start living his dream.

Before he flew back to D.C., he stopped at a restaurant to grab some food. He overheard a guy talking about a house rehab in Atlanta. Curious, he approached the guy to learn more about him and his work. Jaime found out that he was a contractor. The guy was well dressed, well spoken, and seemed to be the right fit for the job. Jamie was excited and started to share his dream with this contractor. However, he was short on time. The guy gave him a business card and emailed him his portfolio. They had further telephonic discussions where he spoke on how he believes in excellence and delivering results. Jamie was impressed by the quality of the previous homes rehabbed by this contractor.

As time goes by, this stranger became more familiar and inspired trust. He called to follow up regularly and used flattering speech. He pretended to care about the success of the rehab. Jamie was sold. His fiancée felt good about the contractor and supported Jamie's decision to hire him. But he was still on the fence because he did not know the contractor's personality or work ethic. He knew sincerity and commitment would be the basis for success of his project.

Jamie sent the property address to the contractor so he could go see the project and give him an estimate for the work. They agreed on $70k including materials and labor. The project was due to be finished in twelve weeks. Jamie wired the full amount to the contractor to expedite the process. He wanted to get in and out. He didn't want to waste time. He had a schedule in place. After receiving the wire, the project had officially started.

The contractor sent a picture of a dumpster in front of the property to Jamie as proof that he started work on the property and the clock was ticking. Jamie was excited about the start. One week later, Jamie called the contractor for some updates. The contractor told him about his difficulties having a building permit to start. He used the city as an excuse.

Jamie contacted the city of Atlanta about the reasons why the permit request was declined. They told him that there was never a request for a permit. This news left him confused as to whether he had lost his mind or was going crazy. He contacted the contractor, but he was out of the country. Two weeks later, no updates. Jamie called the contractor several times, left messages, and sent texts and emails. No responses. The contractor even blocked Jamie's number giving him the silent treatment.

Jamie's heart was racing. It was like it was beating 200 miles per hour. Jamie got hot and could not wait to fly to Atlanta. In the meantime, he decided to connect with a realtor in Atlanta to monitor the progress of the work. Obviously, there was none. The pictures that the realtor sent to Jamie showed a devastated home. The doors were wide open. The few electrical fixtures that were there had been stolen. The dumpster in front of the house was full of garbage. People in the neighborhood had been dumping their trash in the dumpster. These pictures were not what Jamie expected. He was torn down. This lifestyle he was trying to create was disappearing. Is this even possible? He could not believe what was happening. He was not sure if this was a failure, a robbery, a murder, or a flip. In this case, it was all of the above.

Jamie had to fly to Atlanta to confront the contractor. Further aggravating such problems is the fact that he was nowhere to be found. When Jamie looked up his business online, there was no website, no reviews, or recommendations. He thought about driving to the location listed on the business card. After two hours driving, he ended up in a commercial parking lot where they sell physical addresses to businesses. It was a PO Box address. What a shock! In his frustration, he realized that contrary to his expectations, the project was completely dead with $130k invested. He did not know what to do or who to turn to. The contractor stole the money that had been entrusted to him and then promptly disappeared. In his disguise, he came with sheep's clothing, but he was a ravening wolf whose goal was to devour Jamie's dream. He was desperate and was screaming for help.

In this situation, Jamie was ok to break even. He vainly attempted to sell the property as is. He reached out to several investors to see if they would buy the deal. He could not find anyone willing and able to close the deal. He had to hire an attorney to help him with his case. Today, it is twenty-four months later, and the case is not yet resolved. Jamie is waiting for a miracle. He is held captive as this has been going on for over two years. He continues to fight a losing battle.

Jamie is going through a panic attack. Losing $70k is no joke. He doesn't have money to hire another contractor unless he takes a loan. Everything he had was dumped into this project. This contractor killed his dream. His hope was gone and crushed. It is like watching his future sinking down. What a murderous deal! He doesn't know when his deal will be resuscitated. Getting beyond this low point, maintaining self-confidence, and pushing forward was mission impossible. Jamie's life was impacted financially, emotionally, and mentally. It seemed like he was walking into retirement with empty pockets unless a financial miracle happened.

Jamie would have never thought about being flipped. He should have been spared financial loss and bitter disappointment. He had the perfect project. He had the money available and a vision to transform the house. He had the marketing skills to sell the house after the renovation. The only missing piece of the puzzle was a reliable contractor. Unfortunately, he trusted this stranger (contractor) who did a great job hiding behind a facade of respectability. Jamie believed his elevator speech. He failed to do a company research to make sure he was dealing with a legit partner. He soon realized that he was flipped. His plan was completely thwarted. Jamie quickly learned the following:

- Do not trust strangers. Have a plan in place to vet your contractors and do your due diligence. Remember, honesty is like an extinct species in today's world. Too many use dishonesties to increase their earnings. They can be hypocritical.
- Look them up and check their references. It is very important to research not only the company and details about the contractor, but it is important to research the company's ethics. Also, follow their Socials. Checking out a company's social media channels can give you a good feel for the company's practices and expose customer reviews.

- Do not agree to pay the full amount up front; a payment schedule should be included in the contract based on milestones in the completion of work.

- The familiar aphorism that "area matters" is most exact with regards to real estate investment. Before you invest an initial installment and put yourself in a lot of debt over a property, guarantee that it's in a decent area. Look for investment properties that are within a certain driving distance from your place of residence. Flipping houses in another state can be challenging if you don't have the right support.

Summary

As awful as it may seem, these are some examples of challenges that several investors are facing in the real estate industry every day. Nevertheless, the goal of every entrepreneur is to create success. The definition of success may differ from person to person. For some people, success is related to monetary gain, political positions, or social rank. They think success is being financially secure with a steady income which allows them to save money and invest in things that will multiply their money. Others define success as having a healthy family they can provide for. It can mean many things.

To me, success is looking back at your life when you are in your final moments and having a great amount of pride around your creations, accomplishments, and legacy, while feeling little to no regret about what you did not do and those missed opportunities. Although, the above-mentioned experiences and challenges may paint a daunting picture of house flipping, all the investors have reached a certain level of success. To quote Randy Pausch, "Experience is what you get when you didn't get what you wanted. And experience is often the most valuable thing you have to offer." The reality is that many investors get flipped by disguised contractors whose goals are to milk and rob untrained investors. These experiences may be perceived as failure, but you don't really fail if you've learned something. You simply pivot from your original outcome. Remember, "success is advancing from failure to failure without the loss of enthusiasm" (Winston Churchill). These examples and the following tips will serve you and provide you the guidance you need to be successful in your business.

Know your contractor

Don't speak blindly about investing in real estate. The common tips shared by all five investors are around knowing your contractor. Do your homework. Research your potential partners including your general contractors. A background check may be necessary. Check their references and licenses. Ask around to find out whether a friend or someone in your circle knows anything about this contractor. Use social media. The internet has made it easier for people to look up anyone and learn a lot about them. Most companies nowadays are on Facebook, Twitter, Instagram, or other platforms. Be sure to know who you are dealing with.

Listen to your inner voice

Do not ignore the red flags. Red is a danger sign. All the investors had noticed some red flags and questionable business practices at the beginning of their transactions but did not act on them. Remember to act quickly. Stop making excuses and giving everybody the benefit of the doubt. Use your cognitive abilities. In some instances, let your conscience be your guide. Pay attention to the details. When something does not feel right, trust your intuition and listen to your gut. It may prevent deceitful experiences and greatly increase your rate of success.

Self-awareness

Before you decide to start any type of business, be sure to know who you are. Know your limitations, capabilities, and tolerance level. How much are you willing to risk? How much can you afford to lose? Consider the impact on your household. Having a strong understanding of your risk tolerance will help you act with more confidence and create a game plan to deal with potential issues. Determining your individual comfort level is a critical factor in the decision-making process.

Preparation

Preparation is vital to any business model. It is a valuable tool in your entrepreneurial toolkit. You must be ready mentally, emotionally, and financially. Gather all the facts and take the time to evaluate them. As Les Brown stated, "It's better to be prepared for an opportunity and not have one, than to have an opportunity and not be prepared." Have some money set aside for the investment. Make sure you have a backup plan. Anticipate the needs and plan accordingly. Preparedness will allow you to lay out your plans, define the pathway to success. Adequate preparation can allay your fears and contribute to positive results.

Find great deals

It is crucial to buy your inventory at a discounted price. A bright buy will give you the cushion you need to absorb any potential left turn. Abstain from paying "the maximum" for properties. Instead, search for purported wholesale properties that are offered at a lofty markdown. These great deals are usually not advertised online or in the multi services. They are hard to find. Often, they are off market deals. Distressed properties and pre-foreclosures are always trusted sources of great deals. Take advantage of garage sales, yard sales, and estate sales to ask about plans for the property. Search "for sale by owner" signs and boarded properties without neglecting to go to the courthouse steps. Use words of mouth to reach individuals who have difficulties paying their mortgage. Also, leverage "Google ads" as it is a great lead generation tool.

Financing the project

There are a few different ways to purchase your first real estate venture. On the off chance that you are buying a property, you can use debt by taking a mortgage out against a property. The utilization of leverage is what pulls in numerous real estate financial specialists since it lets them gain properties they otherwise couldn't manage and afford. Having a great lender or a broker in your network is beneficial. Thinking about unconventional ways to finance the business can make a difference and save you money. Shop around for the best rates and terms. There are a lot of 100% financing options available. You may also consider doing a joint venture (JV) which is a partnership where you share the responsibilities and split the expenses and the profit.

Teamwork

Build a team of partners who have the project's best interest in mind. Work with a selection of people who can help you achieve your goals and cross over the finish line. Success is not an option when you have a reliable stream of partners who have a shared vision. Teamwork promotes strong collaboration, coordination, and great accomplishments.

Mind your business

Inspect what you expect. Follow up regularly to ensure completion of the project. Hold your team accountable to the deadlines and commitments. Monitor the progress of the project. Reset the expectations when necessary. As a result, there will be an increase of productivity, quality, and better sense of urgency.

Thinking ahead

Always have an exit strategy just in case things don't go as planned. Creating an exit plan is part of the planning phase of any business. It can help mitigate losses.

There are things you can do to prevent being unnecessarily flipped. Listed below is a quick reference to what you should consider when flipping real estate in today's market.

- ✓ Have a written contract with a detailed scope of work.
- ✓ Manage your risk carefully. Consider the unexpected.
- ✓ Do not invest what you cannot afford to lose. Hire the right professionals.
- ✓ Deal with people who have something to lose. Keep business and friendship separated.
- ✓ Have some savings in place. It takes money to make money.
- ✓ Never pay the full amount upfront.
- ✓ Proximity is important. Do not to be too far away from your investment property unless you have people you can trust.

Research your potential partners which include general contractors. In any business or partnership, everybody must share a common vision. Harmony between different partners is a must. A business is like a tree with a thousand leaves. They share the air and the water equally. Similarly, all your business partners should work towards a common goal which is the success of the business. Stop placing your trust and your hard-earned dollars on a stranger.

Not all contractors are shady. There are many competent and reliable contractors. Often, people with bad intentions pretend to be contractors and hide their identity to fool others. Some of them might have contractor friends who let them use their license to rob investors. This book is only speaking to those who make it difficult for investors to achieve their vision of creating a financial legacy for their families; those who are passionate in drawing people into an investment scheme by greatly exaggerating their prospective profits; those who are like donkeys in lion's skin. The goal is not to beat up on contractors, but you want to bring awareness to those who have wolf-like personalities and are shady in the real estate industry.

In addition, it is important to know and understand that investing in real estate is not for everyone. House flipping can be an effective way to raise capital. You must obtain the proper training and do your research to find the right system that works best for your goals in this industry. Not everyone will have to face such dramatic tests of their investments; it is good to be aware and stay informed. Be sure to comprehend what's required before you start. If you must face similar financial nightmares on your journey, keep in mind that there are many other things in life that are far more valuable than money.

These learnings may improve your process of doing business and protect you against hurtful involvement with any investment. Regardless of your experiences, do not quit. Don't worry about the opinions of others. Always live by this quote, "Today, they will laugh at you for trying. Tomorrow, they will ask you for advice!!" When fears stand between you and your dreams, when you are scared to take the next steps, when you dare to dream, consider the outcomes and reflect on the potential positive changes that will come to your life. In the excitement that often comes with starting a new business, risks may be underestimated, dangers overlooked, and the uncertainties of being in business not fully considered. Do not allow greed to cause you to be defrauded. Adroitly, real estate investment is essential. The objective is to place money in, allow it to increase, so later on in future considerably more cash is accessible to you. While all speculations require a level of risk, the potential benefit must cover the measure of hazard involved. It's important to note that property values don't generally increase overnight. An excellent example of dark times in the real estate industry was during periods like the late 1980s and mid-1990s, and the years 2007-2009 when the real estate showcase collapsed. Most of the time, property values occasionally beat inflation as a result of the expansion in typical costs of properties in an economy. Remember, investments are rarely guaranteed at 100%. Use caution and think before you flip.

Resources

Potential Benefits of Real Estate Investing

There is no type of investment, be it real estate, or otherwise, that can offer assurance of a benefit or even guarantee for the principal, generally real estate has been one of the most secure resource classes for investors, while simultaneously providing the potential for gains. Real estate investing offers a few potential advantages, for the most part, not related to different sorts of ventures. Here are a few of those advantages.

Influence

One of the most essential opportunities real estate investment offers is the capacity for financial specialists to use their capital a few times over. Real estate investors can utilize acquired assets to put resources into a bit of real estate they couldn't bear to buy out-rightly, but then realize the entirety of the potential benefit from responsibility and ownership of the property.

It is additionally critical to bring up, in any case, that with expanded influence comes increased risks.

Tax Advantages

Real estate can also give a few sorts of tax benefits. For instance, the government treats real estate benefits as capital additions, which are taxed lower than employment income. Furthermore, the tax premise of your investment properties can diminish with time because the tax code permits you to depreciate your real estate consistently. Likewise, if you are producing and generating cash flow from a rental property, you can conceivably appreciate those profits free from self-employment work taxation.

Cash Flow

Cash flow income can be produced by different kinds of real estate investments such as apartment buildings, storage units, office buildings, and rental houses, Airbnb, and more. This kind of real estate business and aspect centers around purchasing a real estate property, for example, a high rise building, and working it, so you gather a surge of cash from the lease or rent, which is the money a tenant pays you to use your property for a particular measure of time. In the case of a rental property, utilize the "1% Rule" when you choose whether or not the property merits the value, you'll pay for it. The 1% Rule primarily expresses that an income creating wealth must deliver 1% of the amount you pay for it consistently. For instance, if you're taking a look at purchasing a property for $150,000, at that point, the monthly rental income ought to be 150,000 x 1% = $1,500.

Tips for Purchasing Investment Properties

There are a few different ways to purchase your first real estate venture. On the off chance that you are buying a property, you can use debt by taking a mortgage out against a property. The utilization of leverage is what pulls in numerous real estate financial specialists since it lets them gain properties they otherwise couldn't manage and afford.

Notwithstanding, utilizing influence to buy real estate can be risky because, in a falling business sector, the premium cost, interest rate, and regular mortgage installments could drive a financial specialist into liquidation if they aren't cautious. Never buy a real estate interest in your individual name. Instead, for risk management reasons, consider holding real estate ventures through unique kinds of legitimate substances and entities, for example, limited liability organizations or limited associations and partnerships, or trusts. You should consult a certified lawyer for their thoughts regarding which proprietorship technique is best for you and your conditions.

Purchasing real estate through a company is significant, supposing that the venture becomes valueless or somebody slips and falls, bringing about a claim, you can protect your assets, and the worst that could happen is losing the money you've contributed and invested in the venture or business. Doing so will give you genuine feelings of serenity since you will realize that your retirement accounts and other assets ought to be separate.

About the Author

Betty Fortune, (aka Alberte Luma-Fortuna) was born and raised in the pearl of the Caribbean also known as Haiti. She is a wife and mother of two. She's been working in the banking industry since 1999 and is currently a branch manager at a local bank. She is a motivational speaker who inspires and empowers her audience to improve personally and professionally. She served as Vice President of Membership with Toastmasters International and is passionate about helping others reach their full potential.

In addition, she is an adjunct professor teaching business management in one of the largest private universities in the United States. Alberte holds a bachelor's degree in Leadership Management and a master's degree in Business Administration with a concentration in Finance. She is currently a Certified Financial Coach at United Way helping individuals and businesses thrive.

www.ingramcontent.com/pod-product-compliance
Lightning Source LLC
Chambersburg PA
CBHW032148040426
42449CB00005B/449